MUTUAL LIFE

Poems, 2016-2022

Scott Lowery

Finishing Line Press
Georgetown, Kentucky

MUTUAL LIFE

*For Connie & our pandemic pod:
Nick, Rachel, Ben, Ashley, and June*

ACKNOWLEDGMENTS

Thanks to the following publications where versions of these poems originally
appeared:

Canary: Inheritance
Common Ground Review: Gruidae
Green Blade: Food
Lost Lake Folk Opera: Inaugural Ghazal, Norma Rae as Honey Bee, Reset/
        Morning After
Maria Faust Sonnet Contest: Emergence
Nimrod International Journal: Conceptual Sonogram
Ocotillo Review: Somewhere In America
Pinyon: Grampa, Junie, and the Post-Election Moon, How Trees Get Their News
Portage Magazine: Door-Knocking
Prairie Schooner: The Big One
Sheltering in Poems, Community & Connection During Covid (Bent Paddle Press,
        2020): FAQ, The Bargaining Stage
Sky Island Journal: Near the Tracks, Village Life
Third Wednesday: Going Smaller, Vacancy
Winona Daily News: Calling the Border
Wisconsin Poetry Calendar 2022: Inaugural

William Stafford epigraph from "A Ritual to Read to Each Other", *The Way It Is: New
& Selected Poems*, Graywolf Press, St. Paul, 1998.

Publisher: Leah Huete de Maines
Editor: Christen Kincaid
Cover Art: *Factual Among the Trees*, ©2021 Emily Gray Koehler,
        emilygraykoehler.com
Author Photo: Courtesy of Author
Cover Design: Elizabeth Maines McCleavy

Order online: www.finishinglinepress.com
Also available on amazon.com

Author inquiries and mail orders:
Finishing Line Press
PO Box 1626
Georgetown, Kentucky 40324
USA

Table of Contents

FOOD
for C.B.

"Come here, but slowly,"
my wife calls from the kitchen:

a sharp-shinned hawk
sits erect in our snowy pine,

all swivel and no blink,
the soft ruffle

of mottled breast in a stiff wind.
We spot her meal, clenched

to death against the grey,
bobbing branch,

stasis and kinesis,
parceled perfectly.

She leans our way,
peering as if we might

race out to steal
her ounce of yardbird meat.

I return to our chuckling stove,
straining small bones

and onion skin from turkey stock,
our kind's habit.

Filling feeders
later for juncos and finches,

there's little left
beneath her vacant perch,

just bits of feather
caught in the frozen crust.

How would that be,
to wolf each moment, raw and whole?

And yet: these well-oiled boards,
this soup, this bowl.

NEAR THE TRACKS

"Lest the parade of our mutual life be lost in the dark"
—William Stafford

If these houses were men,
their talk would be hard lumps
in the gravy of silence:
affects backyard-flat,
mumbling thrift store colors.
Biceps inked in chain-link.

If these houses were cars,
they'd run week-long on empty
then tank up Friday night.
Loose wrenches living
in the trunk, jumper cables
if your battery's dead.

If these houses voted, they'd
just as soon not tell you,
sidling up their driveway.
That clipboard, that smile:
they'd see an easy life
slipped in your hip pocket.

Say *mutual life* to them—
these houses may let you talk
a microwave minute
in their too-tired kitchen.
True faith? Safe in the back room
where the shotgun sleeps.

DOOR-KNOCKING
Fall, 2016

So much depends upon a red tractor seat
jutting from day-lilies, the old iron pump
preserved in black Rust-oleum. I stop, adjust
my smile and ball-cap both to a friendly tilt,
then climb front steps past scarecrow dolls,
Wilkommen stencils from Hobby Lobby.

To the west, I see our village edge fall off
toward the nearby farms, cornfields aglow,
America set in amber: another hottest-ever
late October, unnerving me but not my neighbors.
They emerge ready to fend me off, arms folded
like umpires. Gothically polite, they'd rather not
reveal which side they're on.

                      Two hunters in blaze orange
fold a deer stand into a pickup. One
tilts his head to hear my pitch, then turns
and spits rebuttal. A pregnant mom
wipes her toddler's nose and vows she'll vote
against that lying bitch and her liberal crowd.

These are the tidy streets my children walked
to school. We led the 4-H pledge at the park,
finger-waved from the wheel on the two-lane
into town. I say *healthcare, clean water,* fumbling
for a grin or nod toward the decent life we share,
but that's all lost in the dam-burst:
bile pounds and boils in empty living rooms,
televisions like open hydrants.

I pass the old stone church we don't attend,
the weed-filled lot where the bar burned down.
Probably time to pack it in—on cue,
clouds darken and flash.

From a front porch
up the block, a concrete barefoot boy fishes
for the past in white gravel, tiny flags flap
from geranium pots, and here I come with
my glossy photos of the damn money-spenders,
like some yappy little dog that sniffs the rug
over the trapdoor and rats out its family,
tail thumping. I don't know any better
either: I just keep talking.

RESET / MORNING AFTER

"The sun will rise in the morning..."
—Barack Obama

Yes, and blaze on the glass—
don't forget: a long look
can blind you.

The birds will pour their hearts
into something once
called singing,

while the last fluttering flags,
still golden on the maple,
must come down.

What does the wind want,
but to tear the skin off
the fallow fields?

No matter how sad they look,
it won't pay to keep them—
let the cows go.

Plow the dreamer's books into
the ditch. Get the gas can.
Stand and watch.

INAUGURAL GHAZAL

If only this throbbing tooth would never grind or grate again.
I'll vote for Tylenol: it'll make my mouth feel great again.

The chickadee, wholly absorbed in each moment's hull and seed—
No interest in the hard-shelled nut of being great again.

Over the whine of his ATV, our neighbor boy rides tall in the saddle.
He fills his tank for a ten-dollar bill and gasoline smells great again.

The holy air of the locker room is sanctified once more, thank God.
Now nasty PC's gone—so great to all be white and straight again.

Grandpa taught me how to rhyme on his bony, sing-song knee.
If he hollers, let him go: we thought it sounded great back then.

The young drone pilot, poised all night above her glowing screen—
nothing like rubble and blood to make a country great again.

Big Daddy Warbucks, back in the house, dripping glitz and bling.
He's all like *Let the good times roll*, now that the NASDAQ's great again.

Go find the Comeback King, old Bonaparte in his iron cell.
Ask him how that went—does he still crave being great again?

Pulled from line, a family stands with widened, dark brown eyes.
Isn't it great to breeze right through, relieved *you* won't be late again?

Five hundred sovereign treaties, each one so carefully broken.
Sitting Bull has the talking stick, before you claim to be great again.

Let's gather now, with songs in praise of Justice's beautiful body.
We'll finger-sift her ashes, and hammer on God's gate again.

And you, Lowery, knocked flat by our national freight again?
Look up, observe that thin moon: already growing great again.

CALLING THE BORDER

Please listen carefully, as our menu has changed.
Si te gustaria hablar en español, that option is no longer available.

If you are yourself a bad hombre, or know someone who is, press one, and
    an agent will be with you shortly.
If you are a masonry contractor, or would like to become one, please press
    two. Same for corrugated steel.
Other job creators, press three. Farmers and care givers can expect longer
    wait times.
To hear about exciting career opportunities in detention technology and
    off-road driving, press four.

To share your fears about our porous borders, press five.
If you have not experienced any yet, press six for an urgent message from the
    President.
If you are dissatisfied with this message, call back tomorrow for a brand new
    one.

If you would like to find your detained minor family members, please visit
    our website, which will be updated really soon.
If your loved ones at home have been murdered by masked men using
    American-made assault weapons, frankly, we've heard it all before.
Not our problem.

To close with Scripture, press eight. Have a blessed day.
But first, you have been selected for a brief survey.

Thank you for staying on the line. We're sorry, but technical staff have
    determined a security issue.
Your beliefs and potential behavior may have been infected by dangerous
    sources.
If you look out your front window, you will see a provisional border being
    erected on your street.

Which of your neighbors deserves to be here? Or your family members? Or
    you?
We are working quickly to answer these vital questions. Please report to the
    nearest authority as soon as possible.
All you'll need to bring is your passport, or your state-issued identity card.
Or just your basic skin and bones.

HOW TREES GET THEIR NEWS

Last night, wet snow slapped down
on the doorstep of the yellow birch,
papery trunk plastered, limber
limbs bent low. I watch as,
one by one, each twig slips free,
launching its empty catapult
into the morning.
            Nearby, patient shoulders
of a tall spruce are draped but
bearing up over hidden rooms
of chickadees, their breakfast chatter.

Right, I think: some headlines drop
like fresh cement, harden to fact
while you're still fumbling for a shovel.
            Our red maple spreads
an umbrella of bare bones above me—
by holding still, it catches nothing.

Update: some bored greenhouse god
flips to the Sleet Channel, solid pellets
pelting the slush on street and lawns—
                  my ears register
an invisible bonfire flaring up,
that exact same spatter and pop!

How to take this late-breaking
news of the weird, this
wintry Redi-Mix, with its
            crackle of unseen flames?
No choice: I freeze
in my tracks, close my eyes—
strange brother to the trees—
we listen to it burn.

VACANCY

Our ski trail stretches across white space, the lake gone deep below—
we kick-and-glide to the point and back, our summer swimming route.

Along the shore, snow-piled cabins stand abandoned. A lime-green
bass lure hangs from a pulled-in dock, parked among the bare trees.

Two silver rowboats, belly-up, a tilting charcoal grill. Behind
a blank-eyed row of windows, deep cold spreads into rough joists.

Mice have moved from snow tunnels into cleaned-out drawers,
and kitchen chairs stand waiting around an empty table.

I think of visiting my cousin Susan on our way north—
how she turned to us beaming in the sunny room,

her thin frame limp beneath the nursing-home bedclothes
like some flubbed magic trick: oops, she's *not quite* disappeared!

Since last time, her Parkinson's has been at work
serving evictions: muscle going, nerves going, bones

packing their bags. She needs to think hard to swallow now,
needs help sitting up, yet she's hungry for all our news

from the old normal: the kids, the cats. I leaned in close
for the flash of heat and steel, insistent in her whisper,

and together we ticked through the family names,
mostly gone, reminding ourselves as we smiled and smiled

how good it is to be here still: this give-and-take,
this life, sailing merrily along its surface though

we know which way these tracks must lead, how much
we'll toss aside, how little we'll leave as we tuck

the spare key under the mat, hear the lock click
behind us, and turn toward the white lake.

GOING SMALLER

Days like this, you slip as you kick,
wind again too warm to stiffen the snow.
We tilt off-kilter another degree, or...
it's just a mid-March thaw: no sweat, yet.
Either way, I can't outrun the news.

Yesterday, the radio host asked the expert,
what about a national health service?
This is America. Forget about it!
Across the lake, a pack of snowmobiles
whines past, snarling like misplaced anger.

I narrow my attention to the oak leaf
that still holds on, the laughing nuthatch:
how small do I need to go before
I'm no longer living in any nation?
A full moon rises, factual among the trees.

NORMA RAE AS A HONEY BEE

Since daylight, she's been knocking on doors
in high-rise rows of corn where no one's home.
Next, she'll follow a nitrate trail downhill
to scrappy pastures by the silted creek,
blue-collar lots of coneflower and butterfly weed
as rare as decent housing and a union wage:
back-roads pushed further back each year,
cows thinned out by mass incarceration.
Along the highway, she hovers to watch a guy
in Day-Glo vest and Carhartt bibs mowing ditch hay,
the cardboard No Spray sign buried in his wake.
Gentlemen: your average working bee is not stupid.
She just gets tired.
                         That bit's a voice-over—
no swarm of New York lawyers to call in—
so she straightens her tiny shoulders
and moves on, ready to dodge cars along parkways,
sail the edge of alleys, wherever she can pick up
that river of vibration that still calls itself a Sisterhood.
Last week, she had her Oscar-winning moment,
imploring pollinators and poisoners alike
with those honeyed, fractal eyes.
When the cops hauled her off in their net,
the whole hive hit the bricks and nearly
lost their way home. Now they sit and wait
with their long-odds hopes for a new Queen, crossing
then re-crossing their many yellow-caked legs,

while Norma quietly made bail and got back to work.
One Big Union is embroidered on her DNA.
She's a free-range blossom, a scrupled sting
in that song she hums: Which side *are* you on?
Here she comes now, as the credits start to roll,
overloaded with leaflets, zig-zagging low over asphalt
and thistle, manure lagoons and drainage tile,
our stitcher of invisible thread,
our busy beacon, too small to fail.

CONCEPTUAL SONOGRAM

I am the tare weight on the digital scale of the universe.
I am the most ancient field of study.
I am a YouTube baby laughing and laughing on repeat.
My pronouns are *he, she, they,* or one that I'll invent.
My conceptual parents worry that I am the next inconvenient truth.
They may name me Changes Everything, being pessimists, being optimists.
My adverbs are *possibly, eternally, hesitantly, unconditionally.*
My conjunction is *if.*
I am light-years away and shifting into hyper-drive.
My conceptual grandparents are maintaining diplomatic radio silence.
Uncles and aunts have turned conceptual satellite dishes in my direction.
Cousins are taking Intro to Nature Or Nurture, online.
In a clueless crossword, I am the answer.
Hint: I am smaller than a breadbox.
I am a hundred-year rainfall.
My conceptual parents are tuning up their elevator pitch to the gods.
On second thought, my pronouns are *me, me, me.*
My adjectives are *tiny, enormous, inconsolable, unfathomable.*
I am neither gain nor loss in corporate earnings.
My kennings are *earth-swallower, sparrow-weight, milk-breath.*
I am already dreaming of nipples.
My conceptual parents are letting me be y and solving for everything else.
They are doing a cost/benefit analysis of thin air.
They are comparing apples and angels dancing on the head of an extinct
      diaper pin.
My nouns are *epicenter, catalyst, amalgam, cheeks, lungs, wake-up call.*
My conceptual parents are dreaming road signs: *Caution, Merge, No Exit.*
I am already reading *Hamlet.*
I am a twinkle in the eye of the galaxy.
My interjection is *Not Yet.*
My verbs are *invade, transform, up-chuck, nuzzle, tickle.*
I am already giggling.

GRUIDAE

By the time they arrive, they've fattened
and partnered on cornfield dance-floors,
then flown high and fast, maybe

fifteen hundred miles. We only guess
they're back, when mornings fog up
and dirty snow softens to muck

in the stubble down by the creek, scenery
gray as their family name. They home
to where they've been before, perhaps

since the Pleistocene, to stitch
an invisible nest, lay low, and quietly
raise their colt on bugs and grubs.

By June they'll reappear on family strolls:
effusive wings and snaky neck, Big Bird's
drab cousins, pointing sharp parental

spears to show Junior the food-life
crawling at his hay-fork feet. Then maybe
we'll hear the creaky screen-door

of their call, the speech of creatures grown
used to silence, whose blending in is all
that saves them from saber-tooth or shotgun,

and yet sometimes they just can't help it:
beneath that dapper splash of a red cap
they open the rusty hinges of their bills

and though nobody would call it song,
we can parse a narrative, like how it feels
to throw yourself into the naked air

beyond any vestige of refuge, then pull
and pull on your long oars until you
finally feel the breath of the curving earth

lift you up into a wild spiral of wings.

CAFE GIRL MEETS BUTTERFLY III

*after two student art show pieces, pen and ink by Echo Henn and cut
paper by Dani Loomis*

These cafe chairs knife at her shoulder blades—
they're made for pain, she knows,
then thinks of that butterfly this morning,
its ornate veins traced, sliced, spread flat
in the decorator's pattern-book
on a field of impossible stems and leaves.
She squints to picture its perfect niche
within her condo's dense ecology—
the half-bath linen? The breakfast china?
With a neon nail, she'd like to trace
those twining, razored curves
or coolly flex each cardstock wing,
admiring the helpful absence of tint so that
it's all about outline: mostly void, a doily
of lobes and capillaries, tessellated
like teardrops. Blink.
                        For a single wing-flap
moment, she sees its paisley pattern
slapped on a rock wall like a living silkscreen,
inked in frack slurry, oil spill, firestorm.

No, absolutely not. She jabs her phone,
then one last gulp of chai as she uncurls,
tugs on her beret, late for yoga.
Across the street behind her, a man
lies prone beneath church windows,
swaddled in moist blankets. Pupal stage
of an unknown species, he's in her
blind spot, also known as the actual world—
crowd-sourced flora and fauna, streaming live.

INHERITANCE

Late summer has smoldered into September, baking the long grasses to a
    weightless, golden glow.
Brass plaques shimmer at the Badlands overlook, hot enough to raise
    blisters,
and dirt-blue haze hangs like a sour mood on the endless ranches, darkening
    the Black Hills, blurring the Bighorns.
When we re-fuel, the breeze that skids across the blacktop brings a quick
    whiff of evening campfires.
Still, it takes all day under an absent sky to sink in: ever since Sioux Falls, the
    West's been burning.

By the time the Clark Fork leads the highway up toward switchbacks thick
    with bone-dry Douglas Fir,
the gap-toothed Absaroka peaks are completely gone, though we sense
    their gray hulks looming like absent gods
above our ant-line crawl through russet fields: late vacationers, sales reps,
    hell-bent big rigs hauling the national grocery list.
Windows rolled-up and tuned to our own devices, but our eyes redden and
    sting just the same.

Finally, up and over: the sudden cold of Snoqualmie Pass, then three lanes
    of accelerating descent—
at the bottom, you can almost hear the hiss of hot metal quenched in the
    slosh and swell of Puget Sound,
the clank of the working harbor, the moon-pull on the kelp beds, the click of
    round stone.

Next morning, our West Seattle host has swept her tidy deck overlooking the
    fog-bound ferry docks.
"This ash", she says, "is all over everything—that's what's on your car."
At the sidewalk, we see that it's still floating down, in light white flakes of
    nearly nothing, casual as a shrug,
rich in pick-your-own meaning: consequence of excess, remains of passion
    or disaster, the precursor of dust.

Bits of former bark or duff, drifting down on lakeside bike paths, the
    barbwire car lots of Rainier Valley,
swirling like tiny white moths in updrafts around the downtown tech towers,

flecking plastic drink-bottles stacked in their manic colors behind idling
    delivery trucks,
graying the ginger dreads that dance around a young hobo's face by the
    freeway ramp.

Unbidden, a scene comes to mind in black-and-white, from one of those
    third-string Twilight Zones:
in tuxes and gowns, oozing greed, adult children have gathered to bicker and
    toast their father's death,
only to learn of their disinheritance from the falling, incinerated scraps of
    the old man's money.
On our fender, what's left of last night's rain turns to a slurry of ash-fall and
    insect parts.
Beyond Alki Point, rows of shipyard cranes raise their dinosaur heads above
    the stippled lead of the bay,
dimly lit by a red briquette of sun in a low sky of damp plaster, and the
    mercury rising again.

THE BIG ONE

Later, we all remembered where we'd been,
waking to that first look, curtains peeled
for the not-much upshot: so far,

just an inch or two, still sifting down
in the half-light between our houses.
Even then, something seemed off—

it was dull, granular, more like salt,
piling up the way salt does
in the palm of your hand. Afterward,

we would try to picture the grass
being swallowed so slowly, try to
count back the weeks and months.

How long did it take us to hear
the whole silence, its soft
accumulation stilling the very air?

You couldn't shovel your way out.

At first, we still gestured to neighbors
passing in the snow, mumbled
in our homes for the practice, even

tottered out among the speechless—
soon enough, stores and jobs fell away,
traffic thinned, then disappeared

while our faint voices sounded
more and more like the wind
whistling among the unspoken

trees around us. Now it's even later.
An ax leans against firewood,
blade rusting. The bird-feeder's empty.

A man leafs through a book, unable
to sound out the words. A woman
stands distracted at a sink,

washing her hands over and over
in cold, gray water. Her look drifts
to the window, slow as winter flies.

FAQ

How far how near how much how long?
> Deeper and deeper into the night sky, or the space
> from one breath to another, or the opposite of distance.
> As much as a percent of a percent. As much as
> the line forms here and goes to there, or used to.

When did when would when will when is?
> That depends: some models are made of polystyrene,
> of balsa wood, of indigenous bones and tar sand.
> Remember how you'd hold your watch to your ear,
> shake it, then listen again. Now we track the whisper
> of numbers in real time, unreeling tick by tick.

Who knew who guessed who says?
> The President announced in the Rose Garden today
> he can tie his own shoes, and will. Our Founding Fathers
> may have seen this in their nightmares: the mad King,
> the latest Plague. So blame the roses, the take-out tacos,
> men without masks. You still have the right to remain silent:
> our votes don't count, not until we all learn something new.

What gives what kills what stops what starts?
> Everyone's reading again, again. Stealth deliveries spike
> on piled-up porches, while the market prints its own silver
> linings. What if they gave a pandemic and everyone
> and their dog came out to walk in the sunlight, chaperoned
> by small children. In all the unbleached blooming.

Where can where can't where as where now?
> Spring break moves to happy hour at the ICU. Drinking
> still essential, unlike libraries. Ghost town playgrounds.
> Sirens approach, recede, next neighborhood over. Next
> continent, over. Like finished, but over and over. You're
> re-routed, then the map goes blank. Wrap yourself inside.

Why did why don't why should why not why might?
> Because we're all in this together means an ocean, and
> where are the boats. Because safety is a thin-shelled egg
> and we want a look. Because the biped mammals still
> make a tribe: even intubated, even roaming empty streets,
> our eyes meet, our hands flutter up, saying yes, okay
> for now, you too, whoever you are, goodbye, goodbye.

THE BARGAINING STAGE

One more morning of nothing yet.
Into this vigilant listening
                    stiff green spears
have pushed up overnight—
did they say something?
                       Just birdsong
in the bare trees, sometimes a siren.

Back indoors, my hands under the tap
scrubbing themselves red
                    when I hear
a familiar, back-brain yapping
and think, okay,
at least this one I know.

If I learn to love one week after another,
one day like the next on the wide prairie
of what we don't know.

If I hold the worst news at six feet
and wean myself from wanting it.

If we can warm to these new go-betweens,
porous or not, safer than skin.

If we admit we're all confirmed cases.

Then? What's left to wish?
Well, of course:
                another hour, another year
returned to the crowded hall,
the coughing throng,
                    shoulder to shoulder
among our fellow mortals.

Meanwhile, an April wind
                sharpens its knives
as my son heads out to get us groceries—
intent, making no wrong moves.
So listen:
                keep him safe, in his casual armor,
and you can name your price.

UNTIL FURTHER NOTICE
to my granddaughter, April 2020

Lately, we've steered you clear of this bright scene,
the alluring crayon-box colors of rung and slat
and every kind of up or down or flat.
Last summer you loved the big kids' wild careen,
squinting to study how they'd climb and fly
through a whirling circus of glamorous things:
high towers, curved tunnels, rock-walls and swings.
You took in each new trick with a measuring eye.

This coming summer should be your turn to shine,
reckless and wild, beaming with all you can do.
You look sideways at the freshly-posted sign,
the yellow tape, then up to us for your cue.
We can only shrug, then turn to go, pretending
we know this one, and it has a happy ending.

GRAMPA, JUNIE, AND THE POST-ELECTION MOON

Along your block now, Christmas lights blink on,
replacing deflated pumpkins, the plastic undead.
I say, let's see if we can find the moon, so
we both turn, chins up in the darkened yard
until there it is, as if pasted where it hangs
among bare branches, an old face winking.
I hoist you up for a taller view. Down, you say,
mid-pivot for the front stoop where your mom just
strung green bulbs from bush to railing.
                                    Maybe
you sense our breath's unclenching—the worst
averted! TV voices from neighbors' homes mumble
less urgently. Out back, your dad feeds brush pile
to fire pit, and saves me a cold can of ale.

Here's the step-stool, vacant. Up, you say, so
I keep my furrowed hand at the small of your
small back as you coolly scale two metal steps,
then down, pink sneakers inching slowly back as if
from a roof. And up again. Maybe you're picking apples,
I say, so you bring me one: crisp, invisible, ripe
for noisy chewing. Delicious, we both repeat,
turning the juicy word inside our mouths.

In one picture book, a girl asks her Papa for the moon,
and he obliges with a ladder so long you have to unfold pages
extra wide and tall to see him, a tiny man, climbing all the way up.
Maybe you can climb to the moon, I say, and you give
your quick, emphatic nod: you were just thinking
the same thing.
                    This time you're extra careful, descending
from so far, and then you hand me a piece of the moon,
right there in your gray mitten. We both take a taste,
while the stars hold still in their tracks—likewise
the clock of my heart, for a tick or two. And though
the sky isn't broadly brushed a hopeful blue,
though streetlights have the stars outnumbered,
even so, it's like any story worth re-telling.
The wish comes true, then changes, fades, returns.
It's not much. It's just enough.

—remembering Eric Carle (1929-2021)

VILLAGE LIFE

Transplants from the city, we've always loved how dark
the nights are near the edge of this little town,
its few dozen houses, neat and unremarkable,
platted loosely around school, frog pond, limestone
church. Early on, before climbing into my car
under the icy sky, I'd stand for a moment gazing up:
Orion's belt, the Dippers with steady Polaris, firming me
in place. Most of our neighbors are anchored by family names,
block letters chiseled in granite among the cedars.
Every week, the strict bronze notes of hymns bounce back
from the nearby bluffs, though no one's ever suggested
we might like to join. When our haphazard trees stretch out
above the yards on either side, they get sawn off.

We've lived here thirty years—there are still surprises.
Back home after time away, and what's this midnight glow
in our darkened bedroom, shifting and blinking?
Across the street, a brand-new Stars-and-Stripes,
big as a bedsheet and lit all night by a halogen beam
that brings to mind a movie prison break. Cool breeze
ripples the flag and toggles our ceiling's shadow play,
off-and-on, like some sleepless night in a cheap motel
where the neon sign outside repeats its vacant message,
spotless as an unread Bible, or the dawn's early light.

SOMEWHERE IN AMERICA

I knew where I was, though I couldn't have named
the place. Raspberries held the woods back
with green razor wire. Grass gone to seed
rubbed against the silvered out-buildings: sheds,
granary, an old milk house. I stood at each,
laid a hand against their cool, cupped boards
as if saying goodbye. Inside would be all the cars
I ever owned: the tan Rambler, the German Opel,
my grandpa's black Ford Galaxy.
                                   I walked
until I came into the town. Late sun filtered
through elm leaves, the twilight air soft
to the touch. Returning from work, men
stopped with one foot up on curb or step,
stretched a little, unhurried, minds on
their own business. I wanted to approach them,
to say I too love my socket set and claw hammer,
the sad song of beer and baseball.
I too own a box of blurry snapshots
and call it home.
                     The men murmured
to each other or into their hands, lingering
near their pickup trucks, where sulky Calvins
pissed on tailgates. I read, or thought I read,
something in their eyes and looked away,
kept on walking, too frozen up inside
to speak the simple fact—"Brother!"

INAUGURAL
for Amanda Gorman

Clouds the color of ripe peaches, off to the east, up early
and bugling the sky awake. Midway through any other winter,
a pink like that might make us laugh, mirthless and un-fooled.

But remember how long this has seemed, while we scrolled
the red-faced mob in boots and Kevlar, exhilarated as any
invaders. Long enough to sink in, how real dark-money

muscle could show up overnight, unfold its hardware,
enfold us all in flags of liberty and death. Long enough even
to grasp our own rich history of looking down, shrugging.

So, remember this day's arrival, achingly slow, stumbling
like a man lost in his own shattered city, its well-known streets
bombed to ruins. When that man looks up and sees

a fanfare of clouds at dawn, he doesn't closely interrogate
such a gift. Maybe he hears himself saying a word
first learned when an old poet fumbled, then straightened

into recitation. *Inaugural*, spoken aloud, feels
like kettle drums rolling out across a dark river full
of true stories. Somewhere off to the east, a young poet

in a canary coat practices, practices, flying her voice up
through its octaves like a kite. Hers is not the faint voice
of a child, particular, invisible, buried beneath

the smoking rubble. Hers is the clear voice speaking
love back to that smaller one, and to those of us with shovels,
or backbones, or voices. Saying, *Let's start over here.*

PANDEMIC JUBILATE
after Christopher Smart

For I will consider my K-94 covid mask.

For it faithfully cleanses my portion of the common air.

For it is amiable, draped from the turn signal, ready for work.

For it is as easily kept in my hip pocket, and may fold and unfold, tirelessly.

For being featherweight yet unafraid in the Valley of Death, it is saintly if not Godly.

For its basic black patina is suitably somber, yet melds with any wardrobe.

For it stays crisp and dry in winter, unlike its droopy cloth cousins.

For its calibrated tug behind my ears can put me in the moment.

For its paper membrane is both fragile and tough, like any living thing.

For its cupped muzzle reminds me of the four-legged ones, that we are all related.

For it can be used to scare possums and starlings.

For it conjures the pluck of Mardi Gras, singing *Jocomo Fee Nah Nay!*

For it can be pulled up with a dark flourish for Walter Mitty moments at the ATM.

For its filter can be imagined as a gill, baleen or snorkel.

For thereby I can swim safely through turbulent days and weeks.

For it is an early detector of coffee breath.

For wearing it reminds me to voice charitable thoughts and hold others unspoken.

For wearing it amplifies both measure and meter of my breath.

For *No Peace, No Justice!* can project loud and clear through its porous shell.

For inside it there is a quiet cloister, the murmur of prayer.

For the partial eclipse it visits on the moon of the human face is often stunning to see.

For it brings an unseen smile from the food coop cashier with the pale blue hair and startled eyes.

For it wishes we really were all in this together.

For talking within it is like speaking into a tin can attached to a string attached to my previous self, listening from elsewhere.

For when it is deployed and I am enveloped, my heart steadies, and slows, and feels some kind of peace.

EMERGENCE
May, 2021

Yesterday's balm has turned to stony cold.
New iris sway, heavy and tight above
their upturned blades. Soft notes of a migrant dove.
Time now, or not, that flowers should unfold.

Bright rhubarb leaves are poised on thin oxalic
stalks, still weeks away from early baking,
while winter's damp detritus waits for raking.
Even the grass has paused, frosted metallic,

still holding last year's justice signs askew
on their wire legs, multi-colored survivors.
We still parcel each breath like ocean divers,
snug in our masks within the common stew.

Held breath—this joy, this fear, once breath resumes.
The bud wonders how it will be when it blooms.

ACKNOWLEDGEMENT
for C.B.

To my rudder, my ballast, my anchor.
To my how-to-ever-thank-her.
To my better two-thirds,
       my unspoken words.

To my life-saver, my life choice,
       my other inner voice.
To my newsfeed,
       my want, my need.

To my first reader, my fearless leader,
       my next engagement,
       my travel agent.
To my back-up when I'm beat down,
       my counter-frown.

To my one-of-a-kind, my radar flying blind,
       my co-pilot, my coping, my anti-moping.
To my grief's consolation,
       my soul in desolation.
To my heart's First Nation.

To my partner on the late-night shift.
To my cloud-lift.

To my walk in the park,
       my bonfire's spark,
       my nest-mate in the dark.

Scott Lowery counts himself lucky for many reasons, including a lifelong fascination with words. He grew up in Minneapolis, attended college in the Twin Cities, and later lived for nearly thirty years in Rollingstone, among the Driftless river bluffs of southeastern Minnesota. Scott and his wife Connie Blackburn have recently moved to Milwaukee, drawn by the inexorable pull of young grandchildren.

Scott's poems have appeared in numerous print and online journals, including recent issues of *River Styx, Prairie Schooner, Briar Cliff Review, Nimrod International Journal, RockPaperPoem, Talking Stick, Bramble,* and *Lost Lake Folk Opera.* He has been a Pushcart and Best of Net nominee, a finalist for several national poetry prizes, and the recipient of a residency at the Anderson Center. *Empty-handed*, Scott's previous chapbook, won the Emergence Chapbook Prize from Red Dragonfly Press (2013, Northfield, MN). He is also a singer-songwriter and has recorded three CDs as a founding member of the Beef Slough Boys, a regional Americana roots band.

A 30-year veteran public school teacher, Scott has presented writing workshops to young poets from grade school through college. After retiring, he coordinated the Teen Voices Project, a series of writing workshops for teen poets, culminating in live performance and a print collection of their work (*Soundings*, Book Shelf Editions, Winona MN). Scott looks forward to resuming involvement with young writers, either online or in-person; see www.scottlowery.org for more information.

www.ingramcontent.com/pod-product-compliance
Lightning Source LLC
Chambersburg PA
CBHW022056080426
42734CB00009B/1376